Bears

by
illus

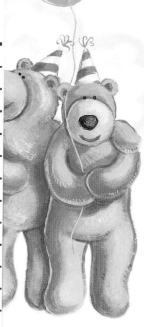

an Diego

www.harcourtschool.com

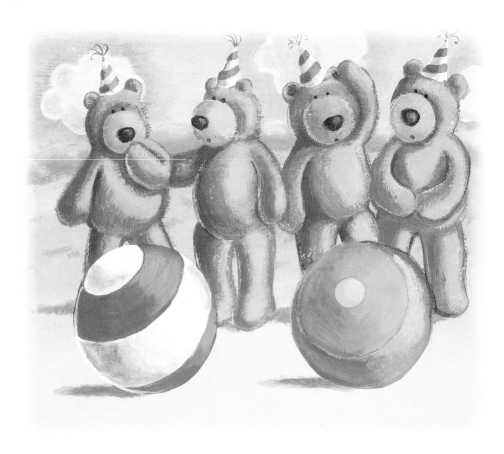

More bears than balls.

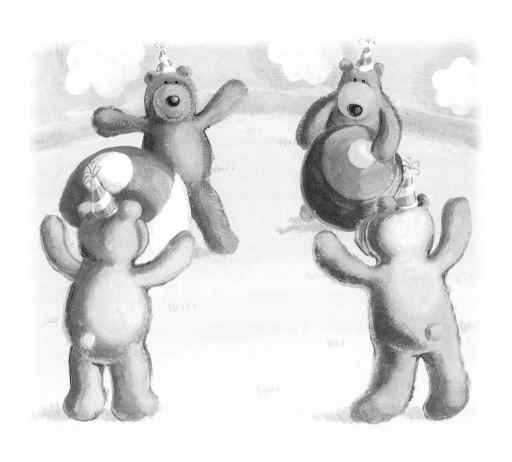

Bears can share!

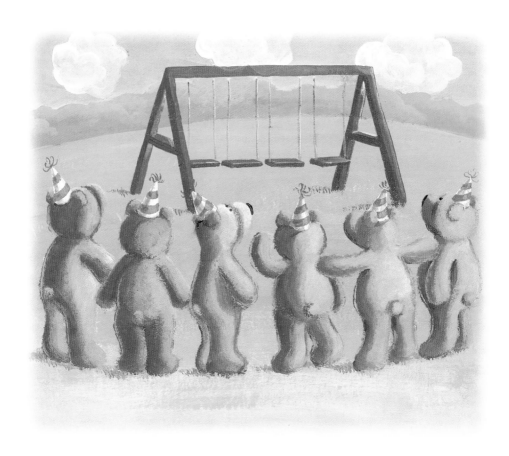

More   bears   than   swings.

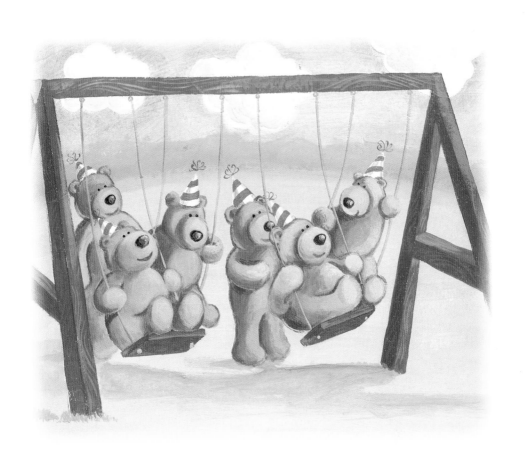

Bears can share!

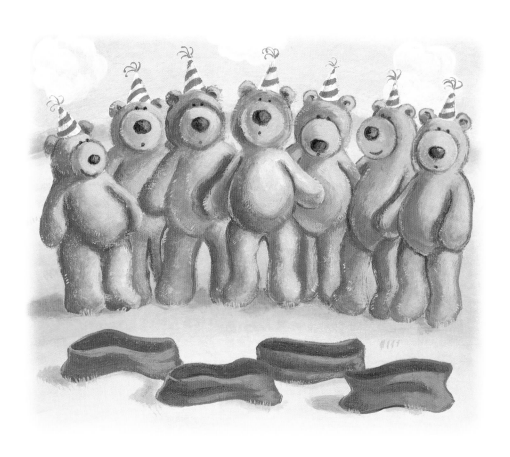

More bears than sacks.

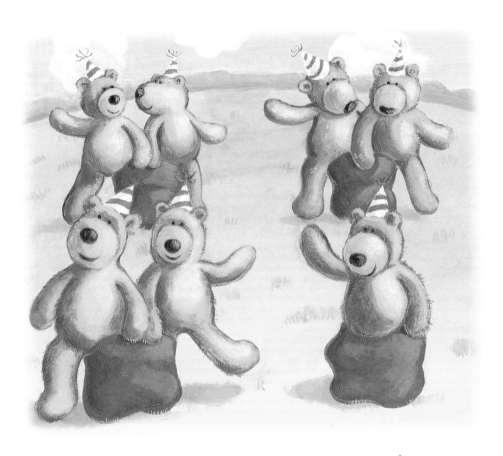

Bears can share!

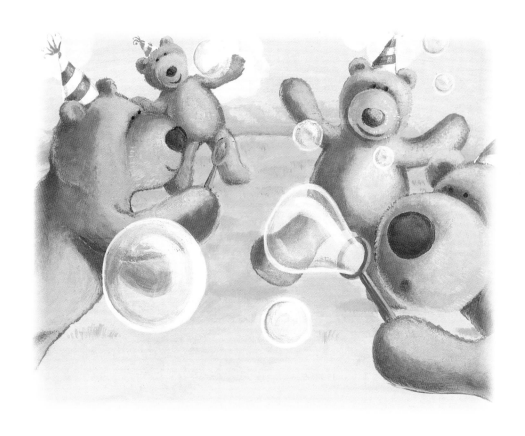

Lots of bubbles!
Bears can share fun!